You're in the Band

For Rhythm Guitar

Book 1

Interactive Guitar Method

COMPACT DISC DIGITAL AUDIO

THE WILLIS MUSIC COMPANY

by Dave Clo

Dave Clo: Guitars, Bass
and Keyboards

Chris Dauphin: Keyboards
Tim Clo: Drums

©2002 by The Willis Music Company
International Copyright Secured
Printed in the USA

Dave Clo Music Sesac

Cover Photograph by
Timothy Clo

Adplate photos used by permission of
jj@astartledchameleon.co.uk

I've left you a message on your answering machine!
By the way,
If a song gives you too much trouble,
move on to the next but keep coming back until you
master them all.

Song Index

Song	Page	Rehearsal Track #	Date Mastered	Performance Track #	Date Mastered
See Angie	6	3	_____	4	_____
Deed	7	5	_____	6	_____
Accord	8	7	_____	8	_____
With Ease	9	9	_____	10	_____
Popular Rhythms	12	11	_____	12	_____
Gray	13	13	_____	14	_____
Denim	14	15	_____	16	_____
Aqua	15	17	_____	18	_____
Blues Anyone?	16	19	_____	20	_____
Every 50's Song	18	21	_____	22	_____
G. I. Girl	19	23	_____	24	_____
Indy	20	25	_____	26	_____
Effort	21	27	_____	28	_____
Effigy	24	29	_____		
2nd Stringer	24		_____		
Ice Age	25	30	_____		
Graduation	25		_____		
Adrian	26	31	_____		
Out on a Ledger	26		_____		
5th Wheel	27	32	_____		
Surf String	27		_____		
Take Two	29	33	_____	34	_____
Climb	29	35	_____	36	_____
5:59	30	37	_____	38	_____
Minor Dogs	33	39	_____	40	_____
Mega 80's	35	41	_____	42	_____
Super 70's	35	43	_____	44	_____
The Turn of the 60's	37	45	_____	46	_____
Blues Any 'Two'?	37	47	_____	48	_____
Low Five	38	49	_____	50	_____
7th Seize	39	51	_____	52	_____

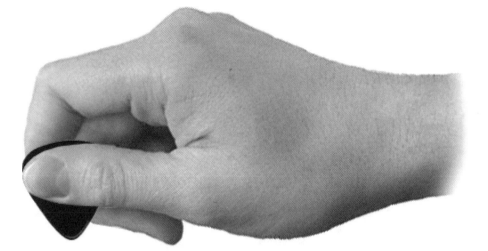

The pick should be held between the thumb and the index finger. Use only a downward motion when strumming until 8th notes are introduced on page 12.

WHAT'S THAT CALLED?

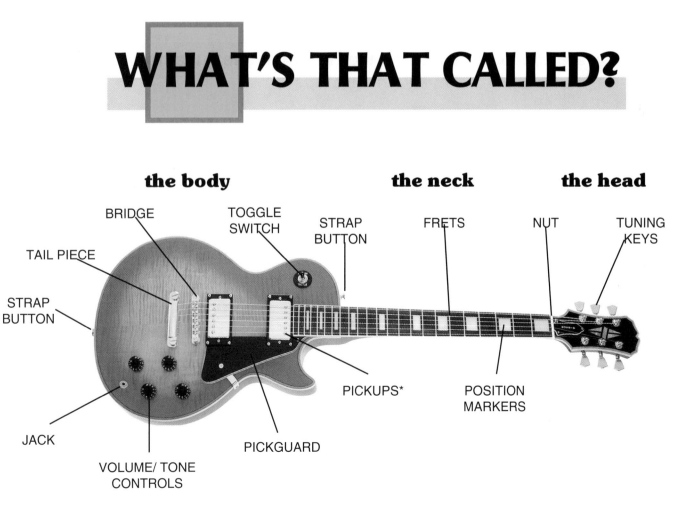

the body

BRIDGE
TOGGLE SWITCH
TAIL PIECE
STRAP BUTTON
JACK
VOLUME/ TONE CONTROLS
PICKGUARD
PICKUPS*

the neck

STRAP BUTTON
FRETS
POSITION MARKERS

the head

NUT
TUNING KEYS

*ACOUSTIC GUITARS HAVE A "SOUND HOLE" INSTEAD OF PICKUPS.

Tuning the guitar can be very difficult for a beginner. Try to tune with the "tuning track" (track 2 of your CD), or with an electronic tuner until you are ready to tune the guitar on your own. Track 2 of the CD contains each string played 3 three times, starting with string # 1 (E).

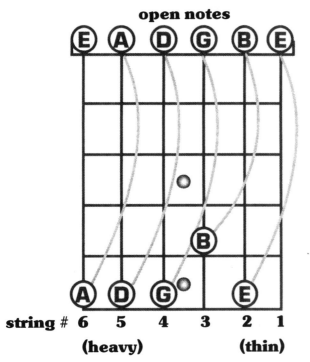

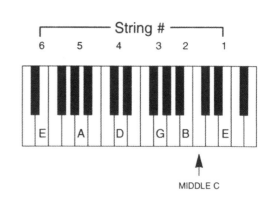

Once you are comfortable with the idea of tuning the guitar by yourself, follow these steps:

1. **TUNE THE FIRST STRING OPEN (pluck the string without pressing any frets) TO AN "E". Use a pitch pipe, tuning fork, piano or any reliable source.**

2. **MATCH THE "E" ON THE 5th FRET OF THE 2nd STRING TO SOUND LIKE THE 1st STRING OPEN.**

3. **MATCH THE "B" ON THE 4th FRET OF THE 3rd STRING TO SOUND LIKE THE 2nd STRING OPEN.**

4. **MATCH THE "G" ON THE 5th FRET OF THE 4th STRING TO SOUND LIKE THE 3rd STRING OPEN.**

5. **MATCH THE "D" ON THE 5th FRET OF THE 5th STRING TO SOUND LIKE THE 4th STRING OPEN.**

6. **MATCH THE "A" ON THE 5th FRET OF THE 6th STRING TO SOUND LIKE THE 5th STRING OPEN.**

7. **PLAY YOUR GUITAR. IT SHOULD BE IN TUNE.**

These CD icons contain the track numbers for your 'Rehearsal' and 'Performance' for each new piece.

Romance aus
"Les Jeux Interdits"

Anonym
TablEdited by D.Meineke
d.meineke@web.de

Strumming - at first, most strumming will be notated by a slash with the chord written above, here's an example of 2 **measures:**

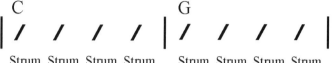

C   G

| / / / / | / / / / |

Strum Strum Strum Strum   Strum Strum Strum Strum

Whole Note Strums
Also known as **"Diamonds"**
a strum that lasts 4 beats:

C

| ◇ |

Strum   2   3   4

Fermata
AKA **"hold sign"**

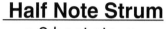

(pause and time)

Half Note Strum
a 2 beat strum,
2 half notes fill a measure

C

| ◇   ◇ |

Strum   Strum
1   2   3   4

Repeat Signs - measures
between these signs are repeated.

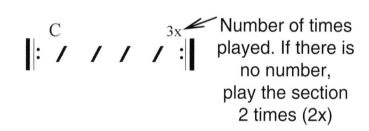

C   3x

‖: / / / / :‖

Number of times played. If there is no number, play the section 2 times (2x)

Chord Grids - a chord grid
is a picture of the guitar neck:

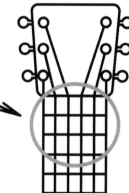

6 5 4 3 2 1
String #

The fingers to be used are written below the grid.
"x" indicates that the string is not played.

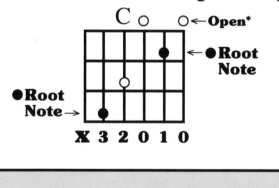

C   O   O ← **Open***

← ● **Root Note**

● **Root Note** →

X 3 2 0 1 0

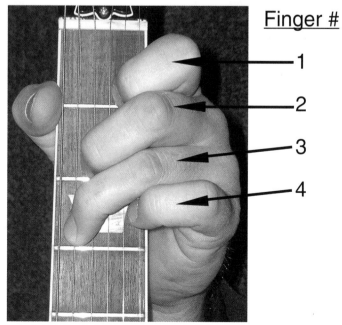

Finger #

1
2
3
4

• **Roots** - (shown as solid dots) are the
primary notes of a chord.
Example: C notes are roots of the C chord.

---

* Open - A string that is strummed
but with **no** fingering.

12612

Chords

Major Chords

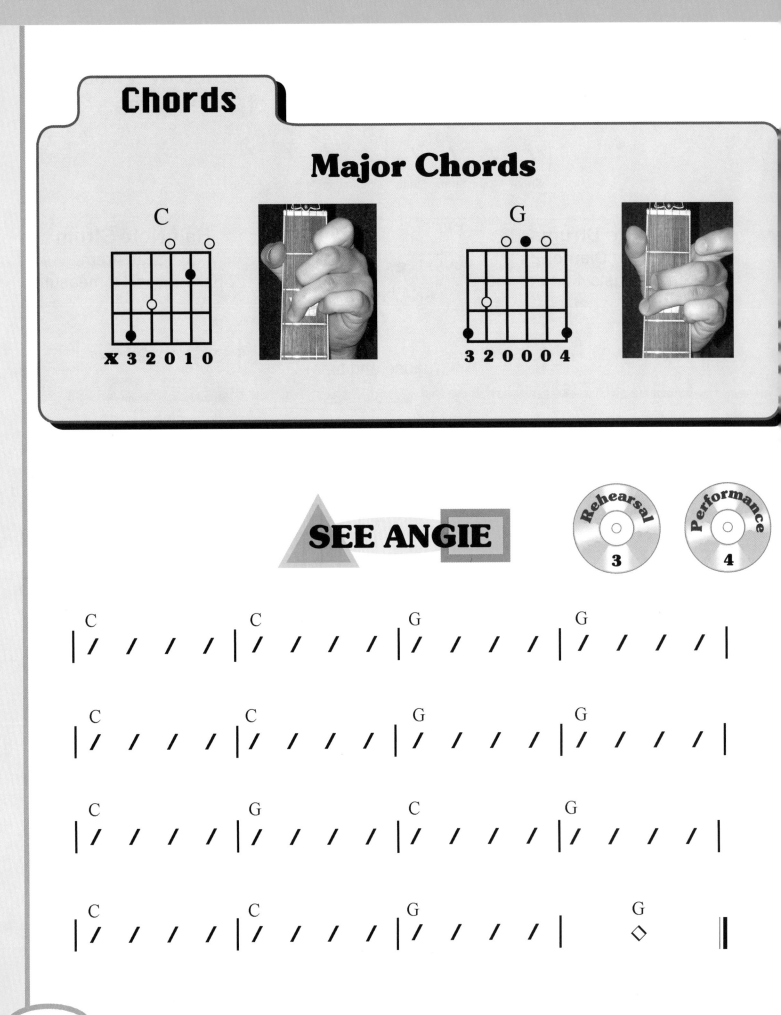

C

X 3 2 0 1 0

G

3 2 0 0 0 4

▲ SEE ANGIE

Rehearsal 3

Performance 4

| C | C | G | G |

| C | C | G | G |

| C | G | C | G |

| C | C | G | G |

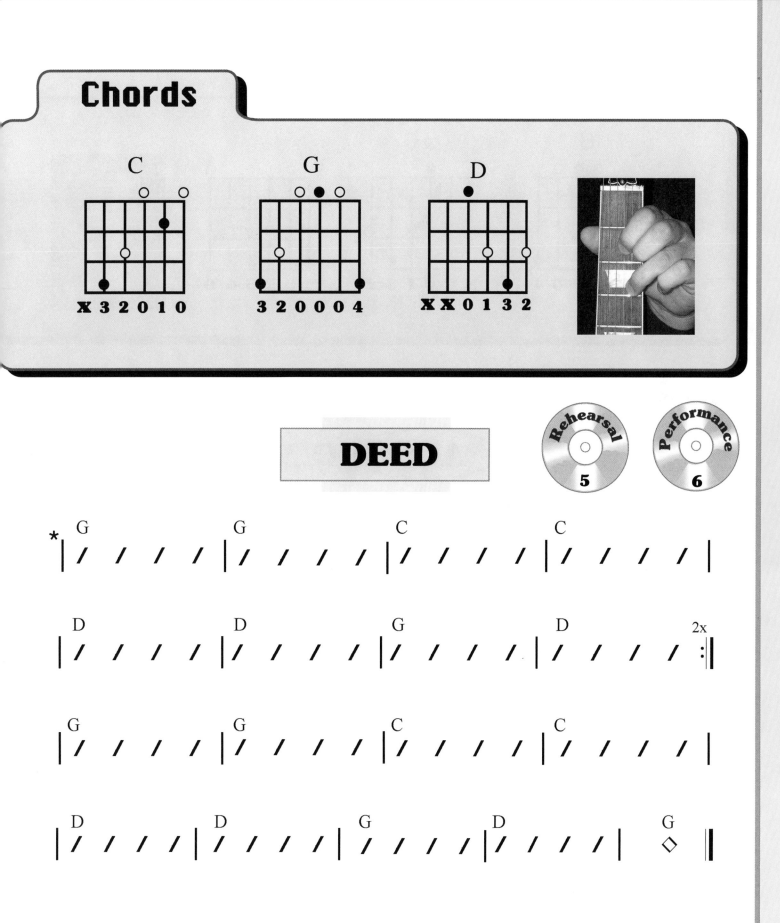

DEED

Rehearsal 5

Performance 6

* If there is no repeat sign at the front of a section, go all the way back to the beginning of the song.

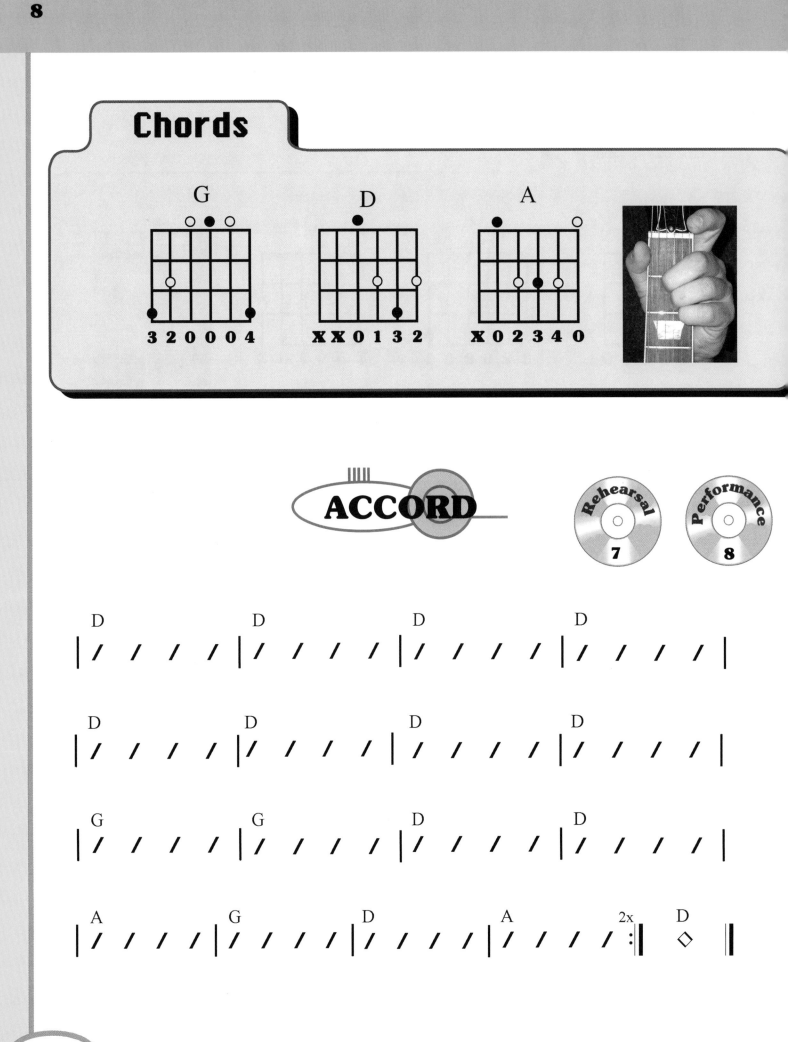

Chords

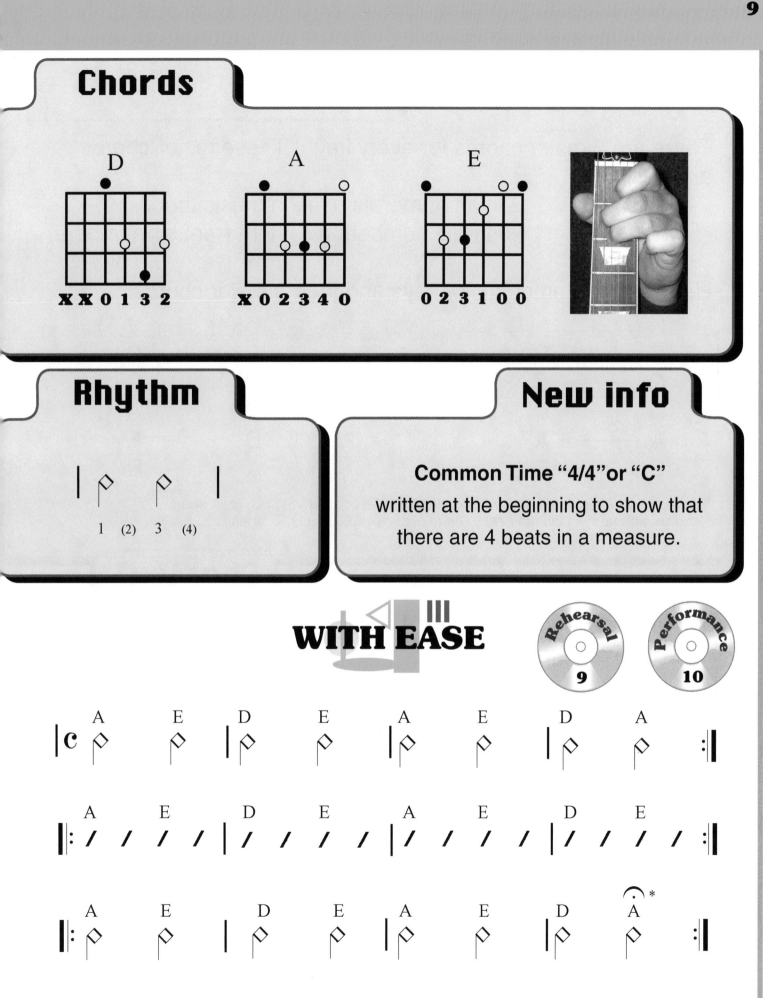

D
X X 0 1 3 2

A
X 0 2 3 4 0

E
0 2 3 1 0 0

Rhythm

1　(2)　3　(4)

New info

Common Time "4/4" or "C"
written at the beginning to show that
there are 4 beats in a measure.

WITH EASE

Rehearsal 9

Performance 10

A	E	D	E	A	E	D	A

A	E	D	E	A	E	D	E

A	E	D	E	A	E	D	A*

* Hold the 2nd time (after repeating) to end the song.

Theory Lesson

There are 3 major chords for every key*. These major chords**
are called:

I, IV and V   Roman numerals used in music theory
1,4 and 5   Nashville numbering system (regular numbers)

Here are 5 common major keys and their 3 major chords:

Key	I (1)		IV(4)	V(5)
C	→ C		F	G
G	→ G		C	D
D	→ D		G	A
A	→ A		D	E
E	→ E		A	B

* there are 12 major keys, and each key has a different starting pitch for a song.
**chords with nothing written next to them are Major. Example "C" means "C Major".

Shortcut

The entire previous chart can be learned by memorizing
the "Line of 5ths"

Line of 5ths

F   C   G   D   A   E   B

The 3 major chords that go together in each key can be seen
together on this line.

Examples:

Key of G   Key of A

IV   I   V

IV   I   V   IV   I   V

F   C   G   D   A   E   B

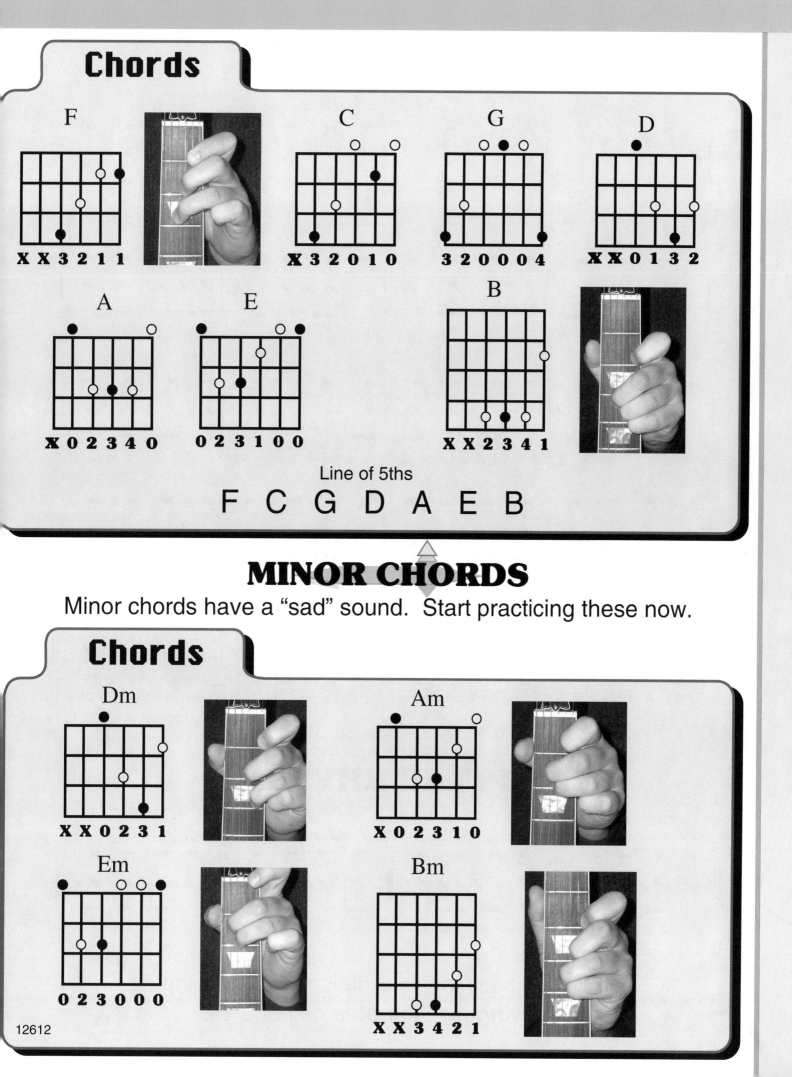

Chords

F   X X 3 2 1 1

C   X 3 2 0 1 0

G   3 2 0 0 0 4

D   X X 0 1 3 2

A   X 0 2 3 4 0

E   0 2 3 1 0 0

B   X X 2 3 4 1

Line of 5ths

F C G D A E B

MINOR CHORDS

Minor chords have a "sad" sound. Start practicing these now.

Chords

Dm   X X 0 2 3 1

Am   X 0 2 3 1 0

Em   0 2 3 0 0 0

Bm   X X 3 4 2 1

RHYTHM

Come back to this exercise after studying **swinging 8th notes** on page 14.

THE KEY OF G

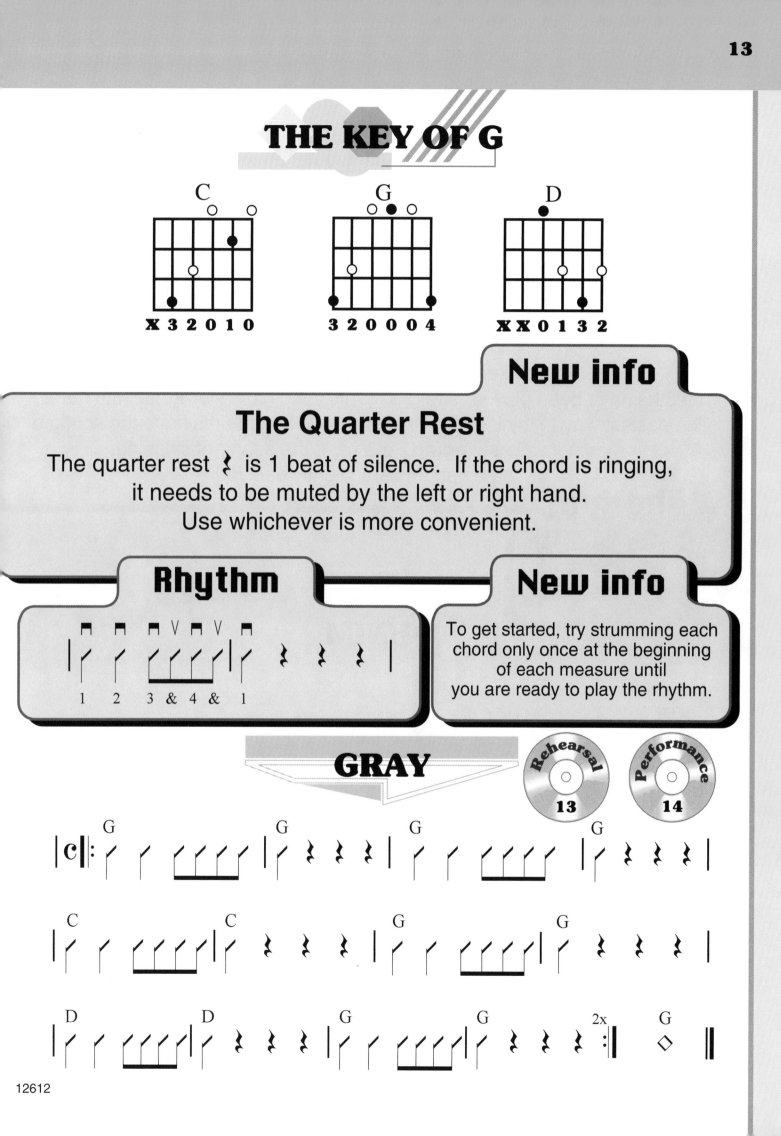

C
X 3 2 0 1 0

G
3 2 0 0 0 4

D
X X 0 1 3 2

New info

The Quarter Rest

The quarter rest ⸰ is 1 beat of silence. If the chord is ringing,
it needs to be muted by the left or right hand.
Use whichever is more convenient.

Rhythm

1   2   3 & 4 &   1

New info

To get started, try strumming each
chord only once at the beginning
of each measure until
you are ready to play the rhythm.

GRAY

Rehearsal 13   Performance 14

12612

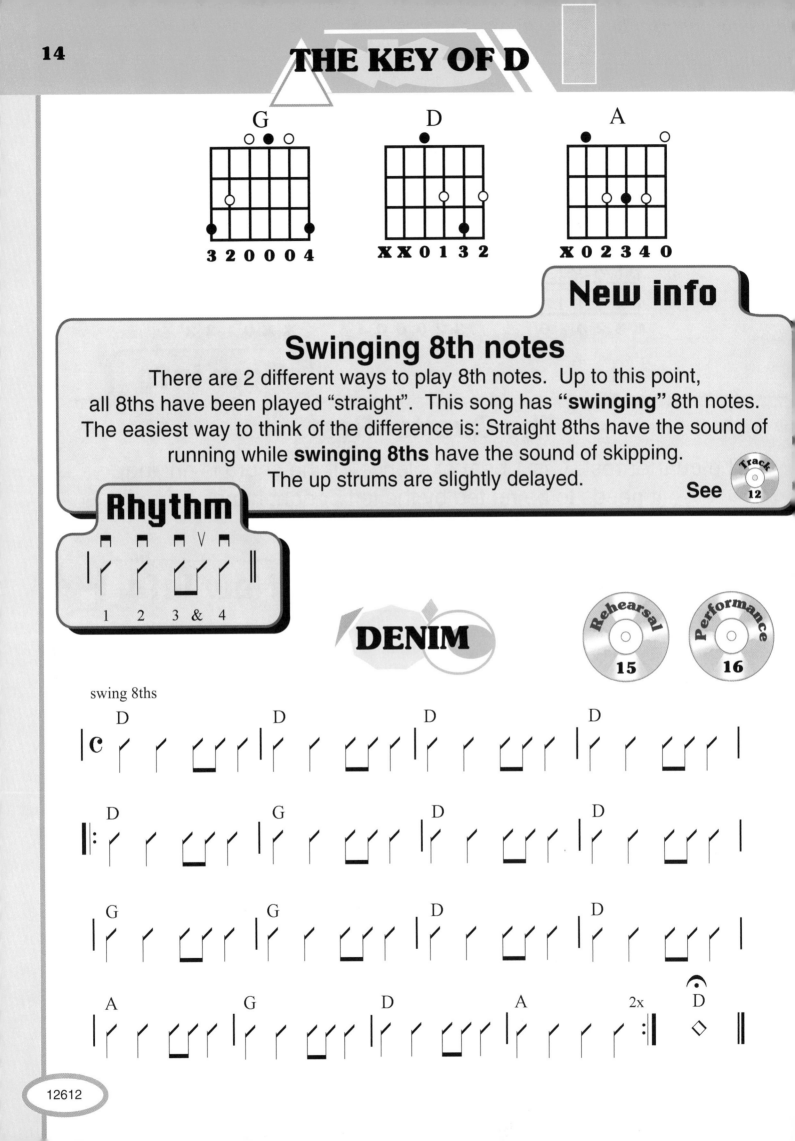

New info

Swinging 8th notes
There are 2 different ways to play 8th notes. Up to this point,
all 8ths have been played "straight". This song has **"swinging"** 8th notes.
The easiest way to think of the difference is: Straight 8ths have the sound of
running while **swinging 8ths** have the sound of skipping.
The up strums are slightly delayed.

See Track 12

Rhythm

1   2   3   &   4

DENIM

Rehearsal 15   Performance 16

swing 8ths

THE KEY OF A

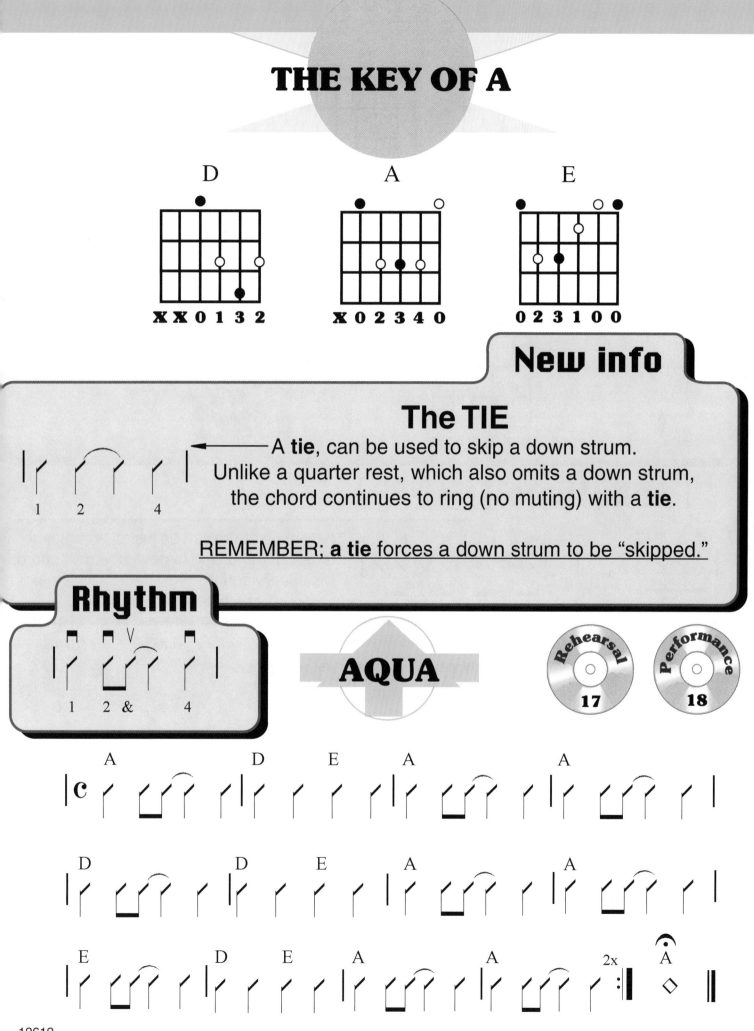

THE KEY OF E

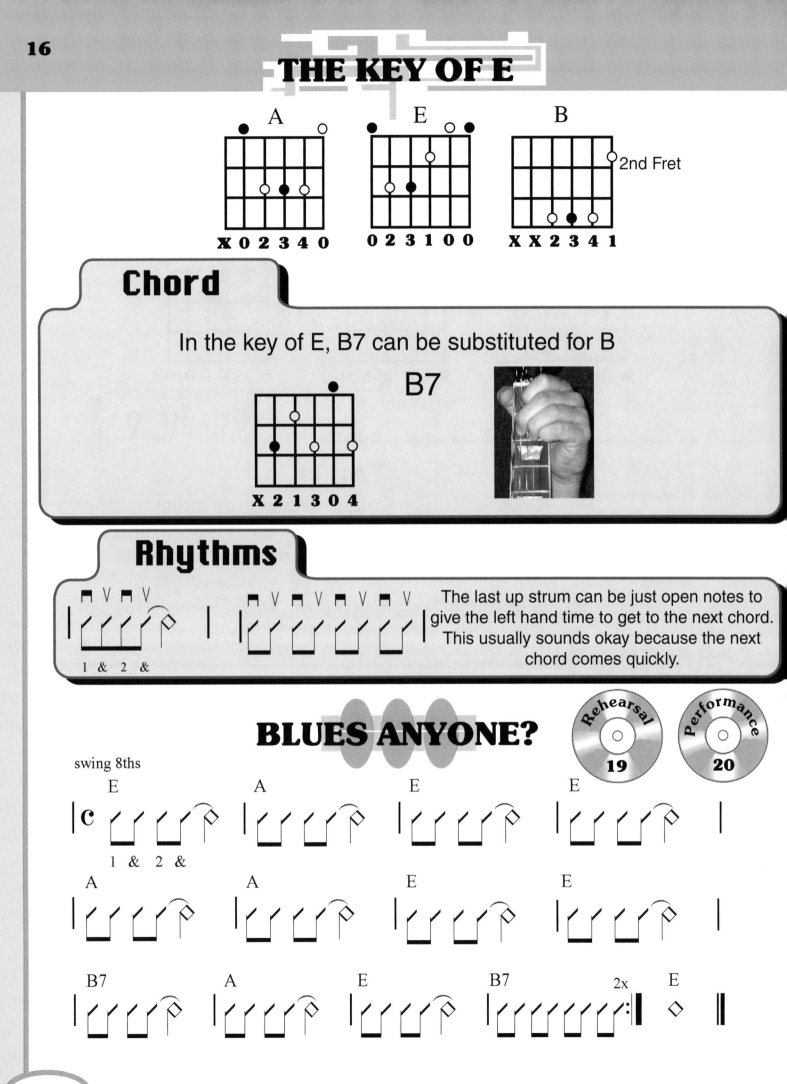

Chord

In the key of E, B7 can be substituted for B

B7

X 2 1 3 0 4

Rhythms

1 & 2 &

The last up strum can be just open notes to give the left hand time to get to the next chord. This usually sounds okay because the next chord comes quickly.

BLUES ANYONE?

Rehearsal 19

Performance 20

swing 8ths

E A E E

1 & 2 &

A A E E

B7 A E B7 2x E

Theory Lesson

The fourth most important chord in a major key is called the **vi** (6) chord. The **vi** chord is a minor chord that is also known as the relative minor of the **I** chord.

Key	I (1)		IV(4)	V(5)	vi(6)
F →	F		B♭	C	Dm
C →	C		F	G	Am
G →	G		C	D	Em
D →	D		G	A	Bm
A →	A		D	E	F#m
E →	E		A	B	C#m

Some of these chords have not yet been shown.

Shortcut

Since the **I** chord and **vi** are relatives, the **vi** will be placed under its **I** chord.

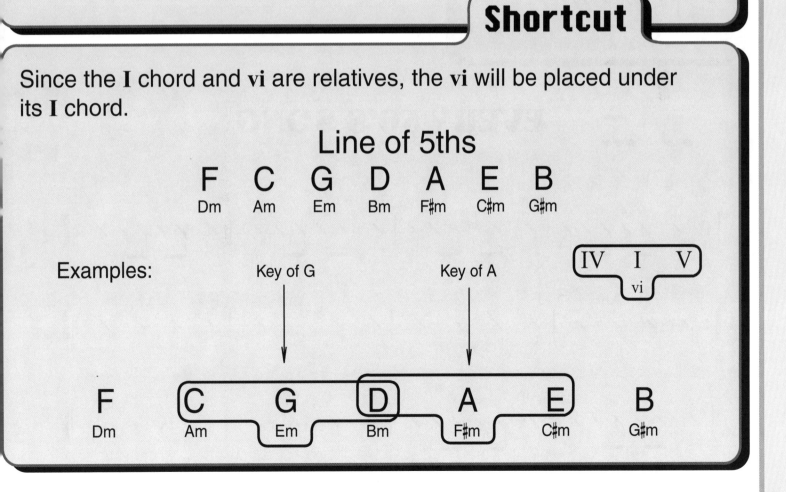

Line of 5ths

Examples:

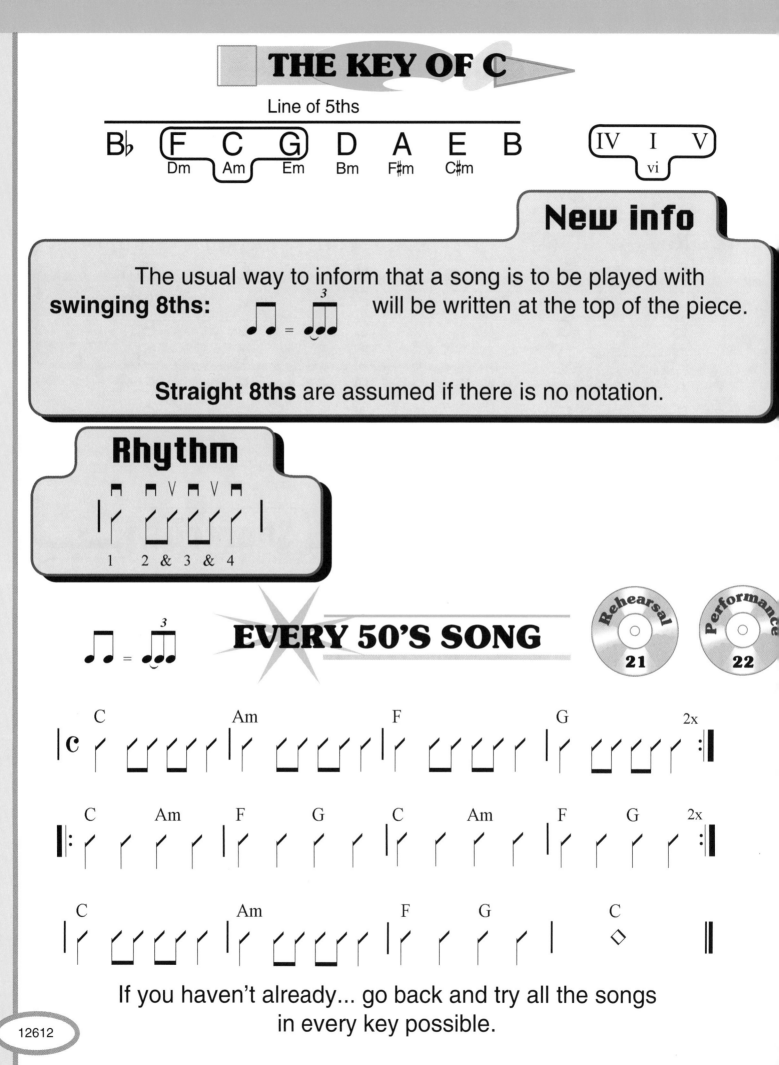

THE KEY OF C

Line of 5ths

B♭   F   C   G   D   A   E   B   IV   I   V
    Dm   Am   Em   Bm   F♯m   C♯m   vi

New info

The usual way to inform that a song is to be played with **swinging 8ths:** will be written at the top of the piece.

Straight 8ths are assumed if there is no notation.

Rhythm

1   2 & 3 & 4

EVERY 50'S SONG

Rehearsal 21   Performance 22

C   Am   F   G   2x

C   Am   F   G   C   Am   F   G   2x

C   Am   F   G   C

If you haven't already... go back and try all the songs
in every key possible.

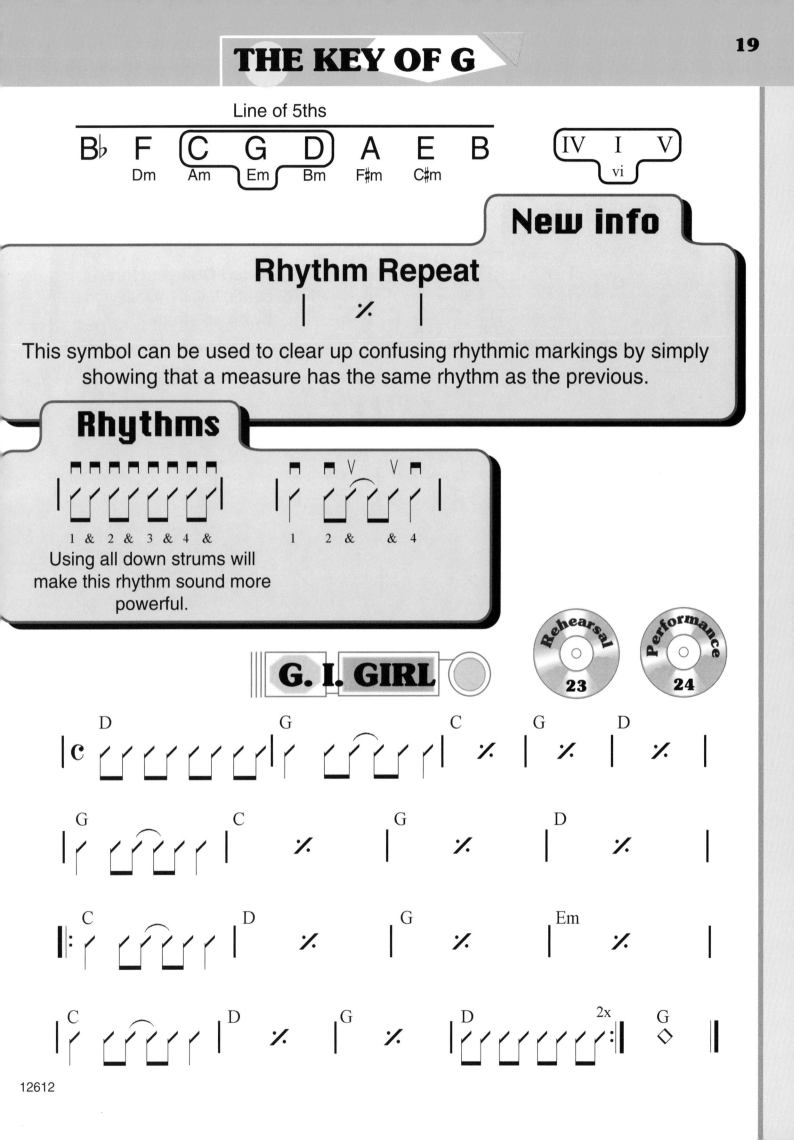

KEY OF D

Line of 5ths

B♭ F C G D A E B
    Dm Am Em Bm F#m C#m

IV I V
       vi

Rhythms

New info

The **Dotted Quarter Note** is 1 1/2 beats. It will be followed by an up strum.

INDY

Rehearsal 25

Performance 26

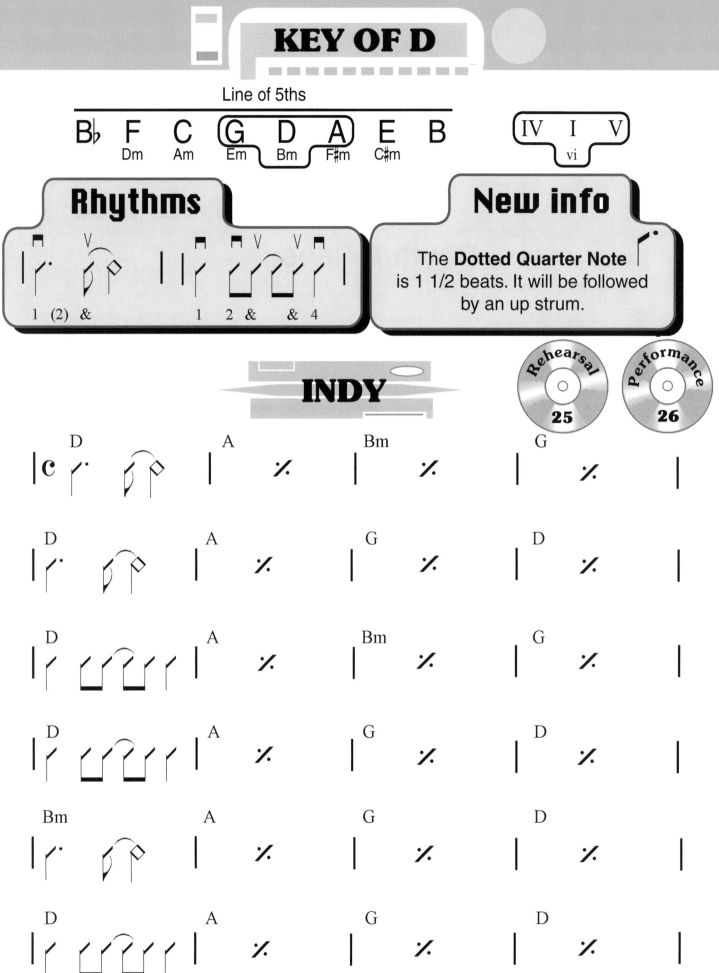

Line of 5ths

B♭	F	C	G	D	A	E	B
	Dm	Am	Em	Bm	F#m	C#m	

IV	I	V
	vi	

Chord

The **IV** chord in the key of **F** is **B♭ (B flat)**

B♭

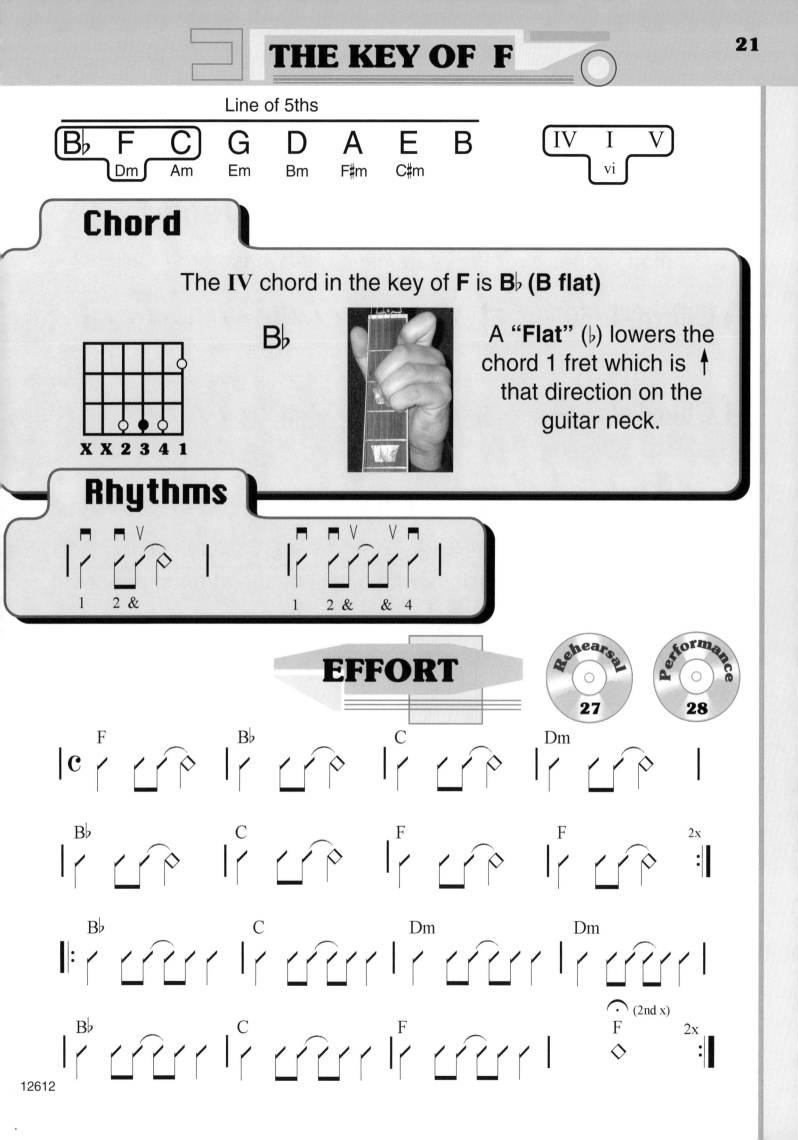

A **"Flat"** (♭) lowers the chord 1 fret which is ↑ that direction on the guitar neck.

X X 2 3 4 1

Rhythms

1   2 &   1   2 &   & 4

EFFORT

Rehearsal 27   Performance 28

F   B♭   C   Dm

B♭   C   F   F   2x

B♭   C   Dm   Dm

B♭   C   F   (2nd x)   F   2x

12612

PROGRESSIONS

A progression is the order in which chords are played during a section of music. Roman numerals (or Nashville numbers) should be used to spell out the progression, then any key can be applied.

Progressions

So many songs over the years have used these progressions!

4 Chord #1 (50's) I vi IV V 4x I

4 Chord #2 I IV vi V 4x I

4 Chord #3 I V vi IV 4x I

Try playing these progressions in every **key** you can.
Also play these progressions with only 2 beats (strums) per chord.

Line of 5ths

B♭	F	C	G	D	A	E	B
	Dm	Am	Em	Bm	F#m	C#m	

IV I V
vi

Go back and **ANALYZE** all the songs up to this page (write down the progressions).
Notice 4 different versions of the **12 bar blues progressions** on pages 13-16.

Chords

More minor Chords

A sharp (♯) raises the chord 1 fret which is ↓ that direction on the guitar neck.

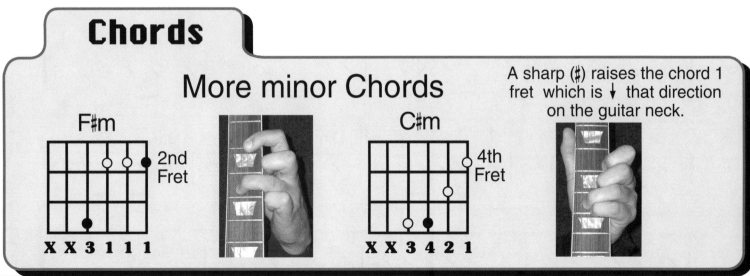

F#m   2nd Fret   X X 3 1 1 1

C#m   4th Fret   X X 3 4 2 1

Theory Lesson

Like the I chord, the IV and V chords also have a relative minor chord.
The relative minor of the IV chord is the ii (2) chord.
The relative minor of the V chord is the iii (3) chord.

Relatives
Relatives   Relatives

Key	I	ii (2)	iii (3)	IV	V	vi
F	F	Gm	Am	B♭	C	Dm
C	C	Dm	Em	F	G	Am
G	G	Am	Bm	C	D	Em
D	D	Em	F♯m	G	A	Bm
A	A	Bm	C♯m	D	E	F♯m
E	E	F♯m	G♯m	A	B	C♯m

Some of these chords have not yet been shown.

Notice: Relatives stay together in each key they appear.
Example: **C** and **Am** are together in the key of **C** as I and vi,
the key of **G** as IV and ii and the key of **F** as V and iii.

Shortcut

Nothing needs to be added to the Line of 5ths. The ii is under the IV and the iii is under the V.

Line of 5ths

F	C	G	D	A	E	B
Dm	Am	Em	Bm	F♯m	C♯m	G♯m

Examples: Key of G   Key of A

	IV	I	V
	ii	vi	iii

F	C	G	D	A	E	B
Dm	Am	Em	Bm	F♯m	C♯m	G♯m

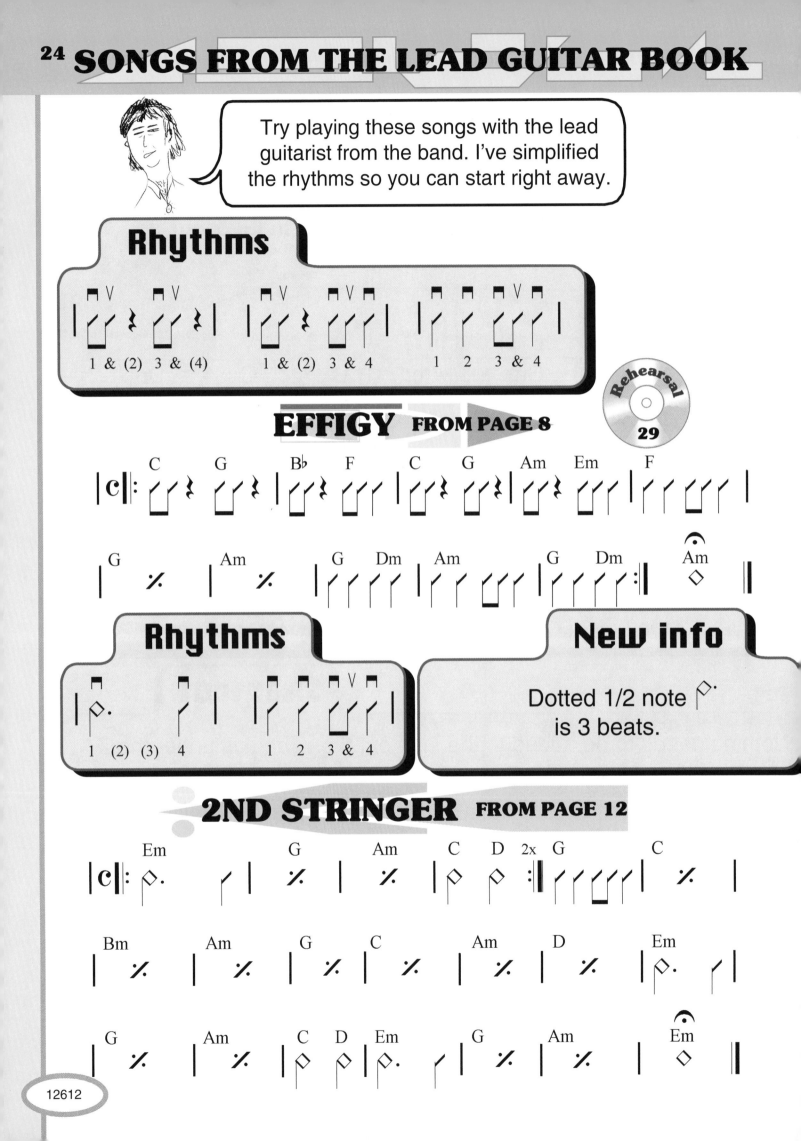

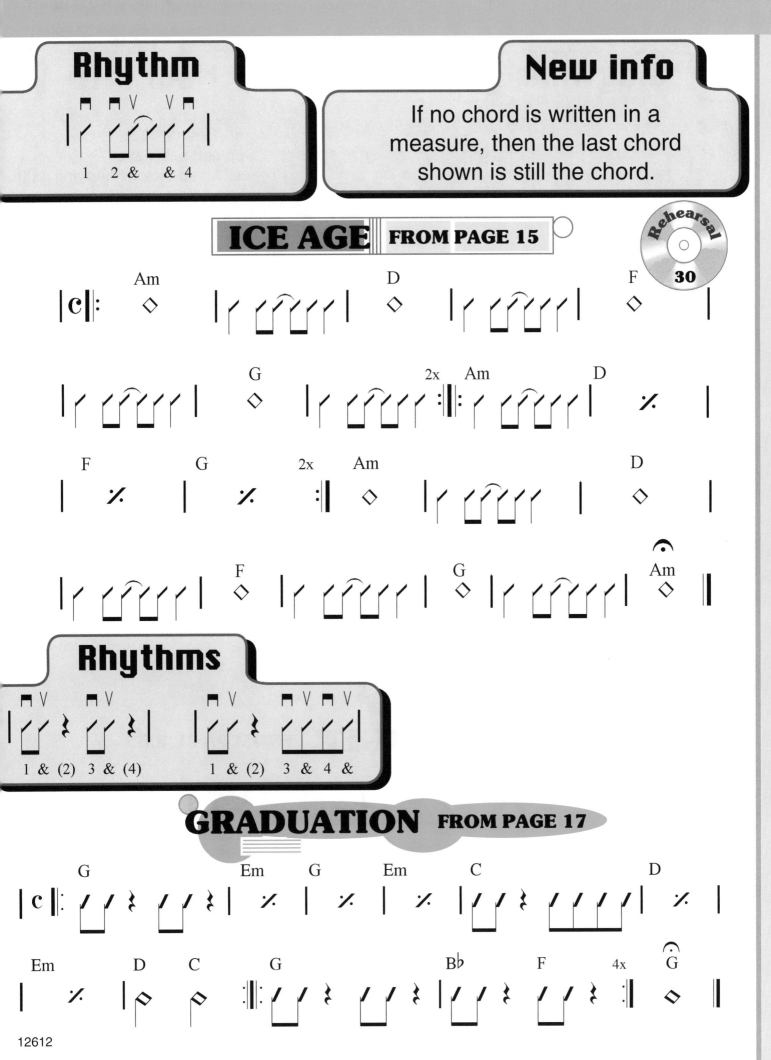

Rhythms

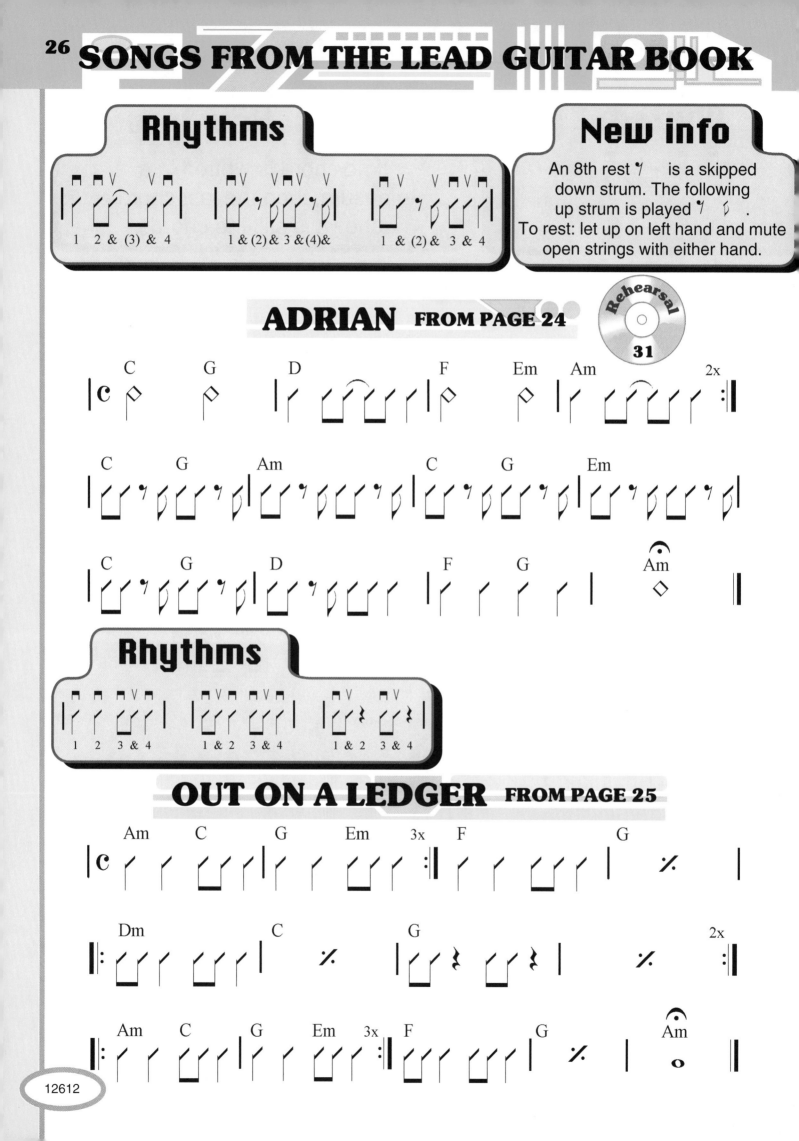

New info

An 8th rest is a skipped down strum. The following up strum is played. To rest: let up on left hand and mute open strings with either hand.

ADRIAN FROM PAGE 24

Rehearsal 31

Rhythms

OUT ON A LEDGER FROM PAGE 25

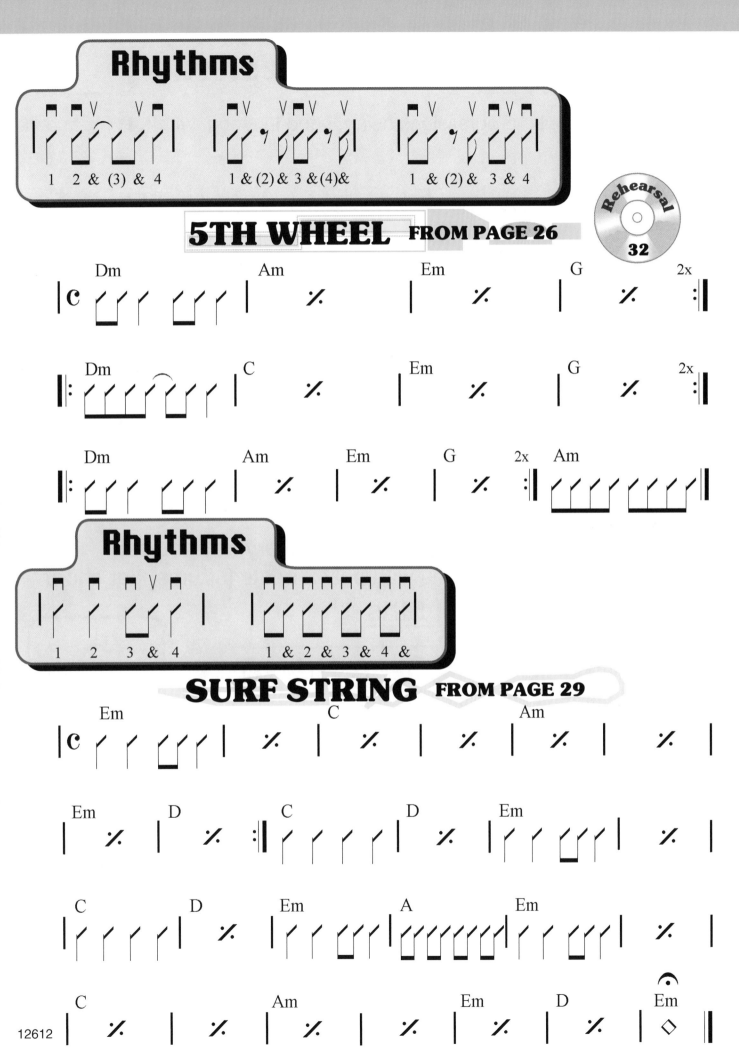

Progressions

Here are some popular progressions using **ii** and **iii** along with **I, IV, V** and **vi.**

w/ ii Chord #1 (50's)

I   vi   ii   V   4x   I

‖: / / / / | / / / / | / / / / | / / / / :‖ ◇ ‖

w/ ii Chord #2

I   IV   ii   V   4x   I

‖: / / / / | / / / / | / / / / | / / / / :‖ ◇ ‖

w/ ii Chord #3

I   ii   IV   V   4x   I

‖: / / / / | / / / / | / / / / | / / / / :‖ ◇ ‖

w/ iii Chord #1

I   iii   IV   V   4x   I

‖: / / / / | / / / / | / / / / | / / / / :‖ ◇ ‖

w/ iii Chord #2

I   iii   vi   IV   4x   I

‖: / / / / | / / / / | / / / / | / / / / :‖ ◇ ‖

w/ iii Chord #3

I   V   iii   IV   4x   I

‖: / / / / | / / / / | / / / / | / / / / :‖ ◇ ‖

Try playing these progressions in every **key** you can.
Also play these progressions with only 2 beats (strums) per chord.

Line of 5ths

B♭	F	C	G	D	A	E	B
Gm	Dm	Am	Em	Bm	F#m	C#m	G#m

IV	I	V
ii	vi	iii

Chords

More minor Chords

Gm

3rd Fret

X X 3 1 1 1

G#m

4th Fret

X X 3 1 1 1

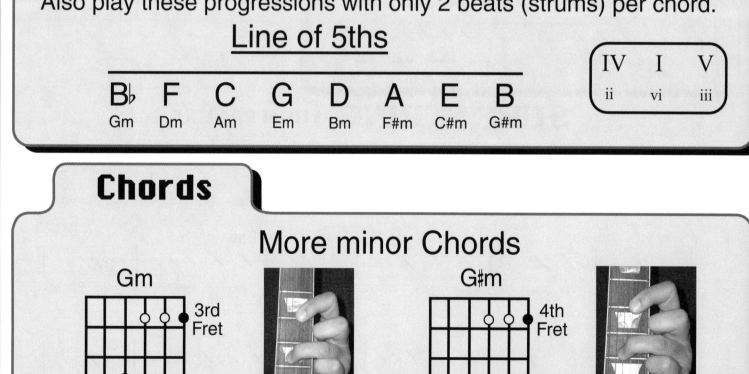

Rhythm

6/8 Time means that there are six beats per measure except that the 8th note, instead of the quarter note = 1 beat. The 8th notes are grouped in sets of 3. (1 2 3) (4 5 6)

Use all down strums for this song.

Sorry...we've changed this song from the key of C to the key of G. Can you transpose it for us? Write the new chords above the old ones.

5:59

ritard. - gradually slow down

Theory Lesson

The **vii chord (7)** is the final chord in each major key.
The vii chord is **minor** ♭5, sometimes called diminished.

Key	I	ii	iii	IV	V	vi	vii m♭5 (7 m♭5)
F	F	Gm	Am	B♭	C	Dm	Em♭5
C	C	Dm	Em	F	G	Am	Bm♭5
G	G	Am	Bm	C	D	Em	F#m♭5
D	D	Em	F#m	G	A	Bm	C#m♭5
A	A	Bm	C#m	D	E	F#m	G#m♭5
E	E	F#m	G#m	A	B	C#m	D#m♭5

Notice that every key now has a chord for all 7 letters of the music alphabet (A-G). Example: The **key of C** - C, Dm, Em, F, G, Am, Bm♭5.

Shortcut

Nothing needs to be added to the Line of 5ths. The vii is to the right of the iii, but it needs to be made **minor** ♭5 instead of just **minor**.

Line of 5ths

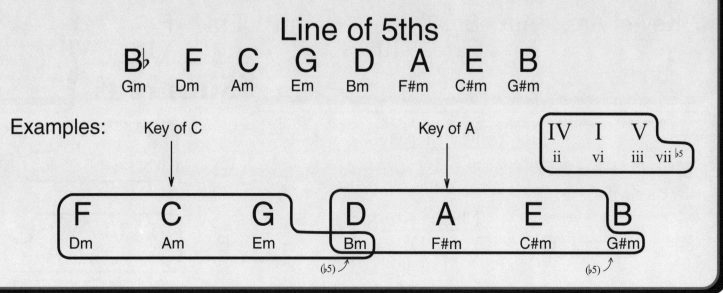

12612

MINOR 7♭5 CHORDS

Chords

Adding the 7th to **minor♭5** makes a more advanced chord that is actually easier to play on the guitar called: **minor7♭5** or **m7♭5**.

Em7♭5

X X 1 3 3 3

Bm7♭5

X 1 3 2 4 X

Let 1st finger touch and mute 1st string

F#m7♭5

X X 2 3 1 4

C#m7♭5

X 3 1 0 0 0

Theory Lesson

Minor Keys

All **major keys** have a **relative minor key** that shares all the same chords. Example: The key of **C major** and the key of **A minor** share all of the same chords. The numbering is changed to reflect the minor i chord.

Key of C:	C	Dm	Em	F	G	Am	Bm♭5
	I	ii	iii	IV	V	vi	vii♭5

Key of Am:	Am	Bm♭5	C	Dm	Em	F	G
	i	iim♭5	III	iv	v	VI	VII

Shortcut

Major Keys

B♭	F	C	G	D	A	E	B
Gm	Dm	Am	Em	Bm	F#m	C#m	G#m

IV	I	V		
ii	vi	iii	vii♭5	

Minor Keys

B♭	F	C	G	D	A	E	B
Gm	Dm	Am	Em	Bm	F#m	C#m	G#m

VI	III	VII		
iv	i	v	ii♭5	

Same chords different numbers

Theory Lesson

Minor keys have the option of having a **minor** or **major** V chord.
The chords in the key of **Am** with the Major V chord are:

i	iim7♭5	III	iv	**V**	VI	VII
Am	Bm♭5	C	Dm	**E**	F	G

In the case of a **major V**, the <u>Line of 5ths</u> looks like this for the key of **Am**:

B♭	F	C	G	D	A	E	VI	III	VII
Gm	Dm	Am	E→	Bm7♭5	F#m	C#m	iv	i	V iim7♭5

(Major)

Rhythm

⊓ ⊓ ⊓ V ⊓ ⊓

1 2 3 & 4

half rest   whole rest

Progression

i	VII	VI	V

| / / / / | / / / / |

MINOR DOGS

♪♪ = ♪♪♪ (3)

Rehearsal **39**   Performance **40**

Am G F E Am G F E

Am G F E Am

Dm   Dm   Am   Am

Dm   Dm   Bm7♭5   E
1 2 &

Am G F E Am G F E

Am G F E Am   Am

Theory Lesson

The **vii chord** has a substitute chord that is not really in the key but is more widely used than the viim♭5 (diminished) chord. This substitute vii chord is called ♭**VII.** The ♭**VII** chord is a major chord.

Key	I	ii	iii	IV	V	vi	♭VII (♭7)	viim(♭5)
F	F	Gm	Am	B♭	C	Dm	**E♭**	Em(♭5)
C	C	Dm	Em	F	G	Am	**B♭**	Bm(♭5)
G	G	Am	Bm	C	D	Em	**F**	F♯m(♭5)
D	D	Em	F♯m	G	A	Bm	**C**	C♯m(♭5)
A	A	Bm	C♯m	D	E	F♯m	**G**	G♯m(♭5)
E	E	F♯m	G♯m	A	B	C♯m	**D**	D♯m(♭5)

Most of the ♭VII chords are chords already learned.

Shortcut

Nothing needs to be added to the Line of 5ths. The ♭**VII** is to the left of the **IV.** Sometimes the ♭**VII** is called the **IV of IV.**

Remember: The **Line of 5ths** gives all the information of the above chart!

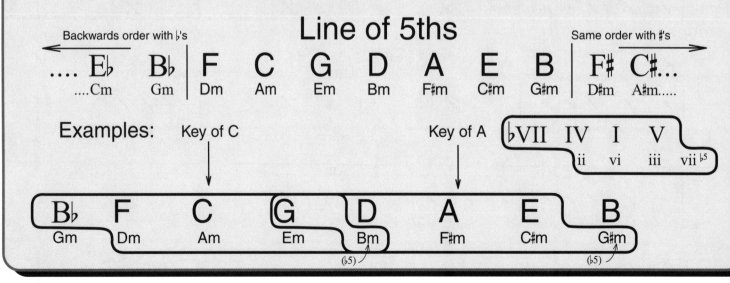

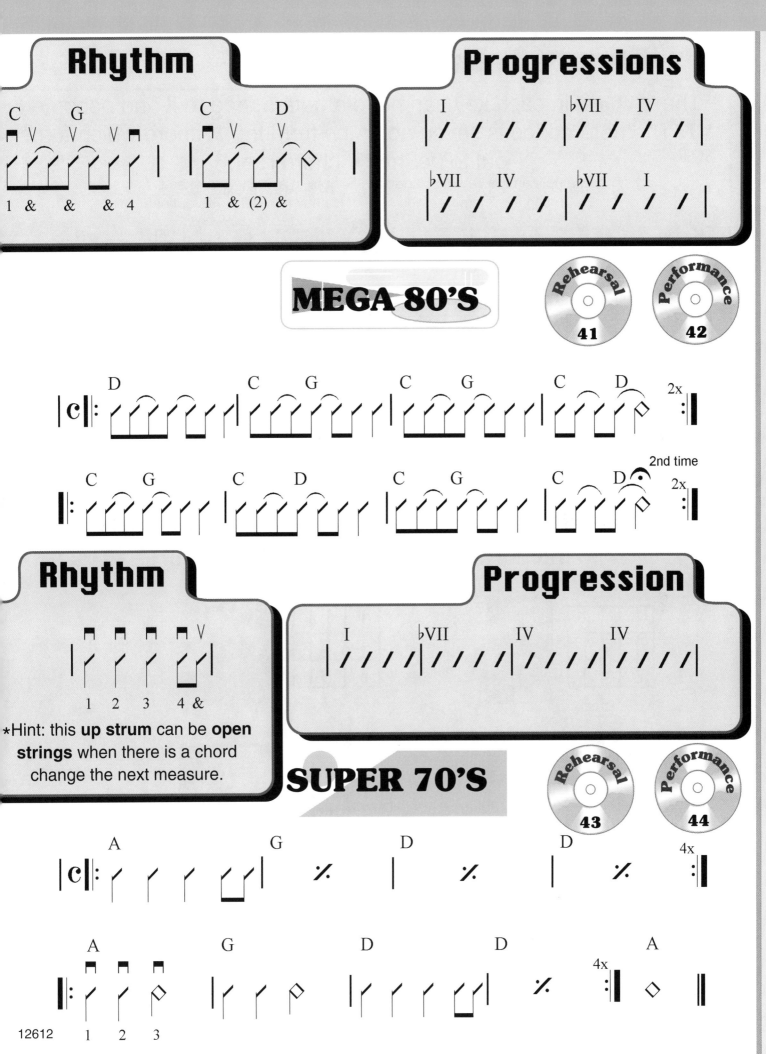

Theory Lesson

The **V chord** in each key can have a note added to it and become **V7**. The note added is seven notes up from the **V** chord which turns out to be the **IV** chord root.

Example: in the key of F, adding a B♭ note to a C chord makes C7.
By putting the 7 in parenthesis (7), it is shown that the 7 is optional.

Key	I	ii	iii	IV	V(7)[5(7)]	vi	♭VII	viim7♭5
F	F	Gm	Am	B♭	C(7)	Dm	E♭	Em7♭5
C	C	Dm	Em	F	G(7)	Am	B♭	Bm7♭5
G	G	Am	Bm	C	D(7)	Em	F	F#m7♭5
D	D	Em	F#m	G	A(7)	Bm	C	C#m7♭5
A	A	Bm	C#m	D	E(7)	F#m	G	G#m7♭5
E	E	F#m	G#m	A	B(7)	C#m	D	D#m7♭5

Of the major chords **I, IV and V** only **V** can be made **7th** without stepping outside the key.

Chords

7th chords (A.K.A. Dominant Chords)

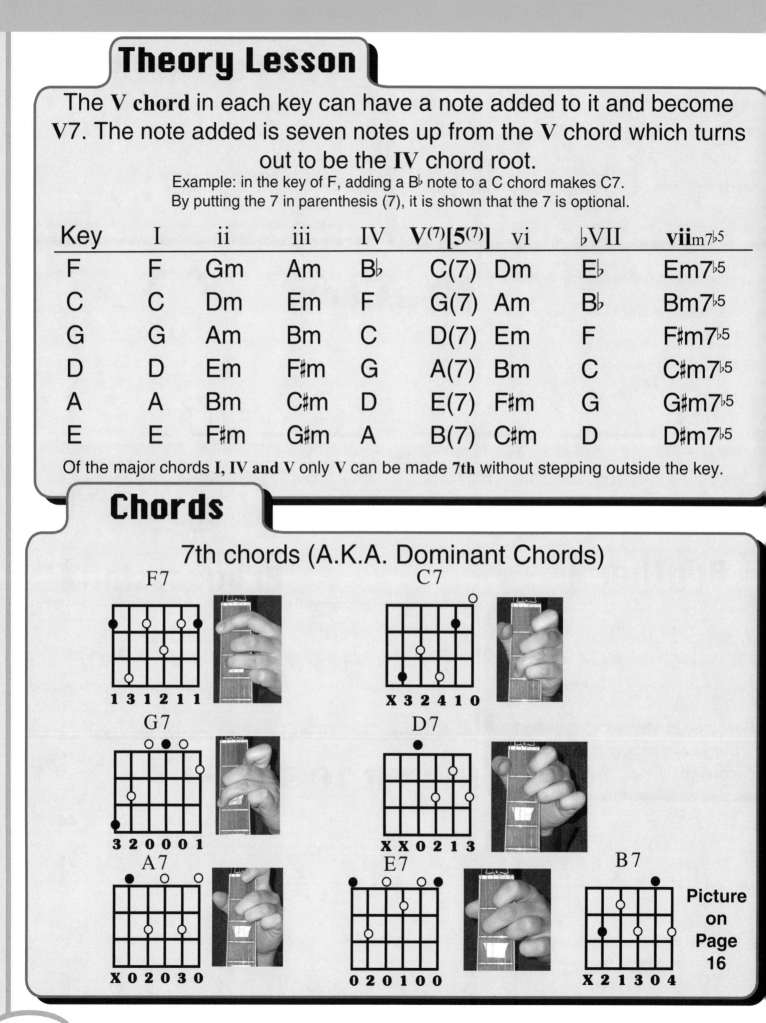

F7
1 3 1 2 1 1

C7
X 3 2 4 1 0

G7
3 2 0 0 0 1

D7
X X 0 2 1 3

A7
X 0 2 0 3 0

E7
0 2 0 1 0 0

B7
X 2 1 3 0 4

Picture on Page 16

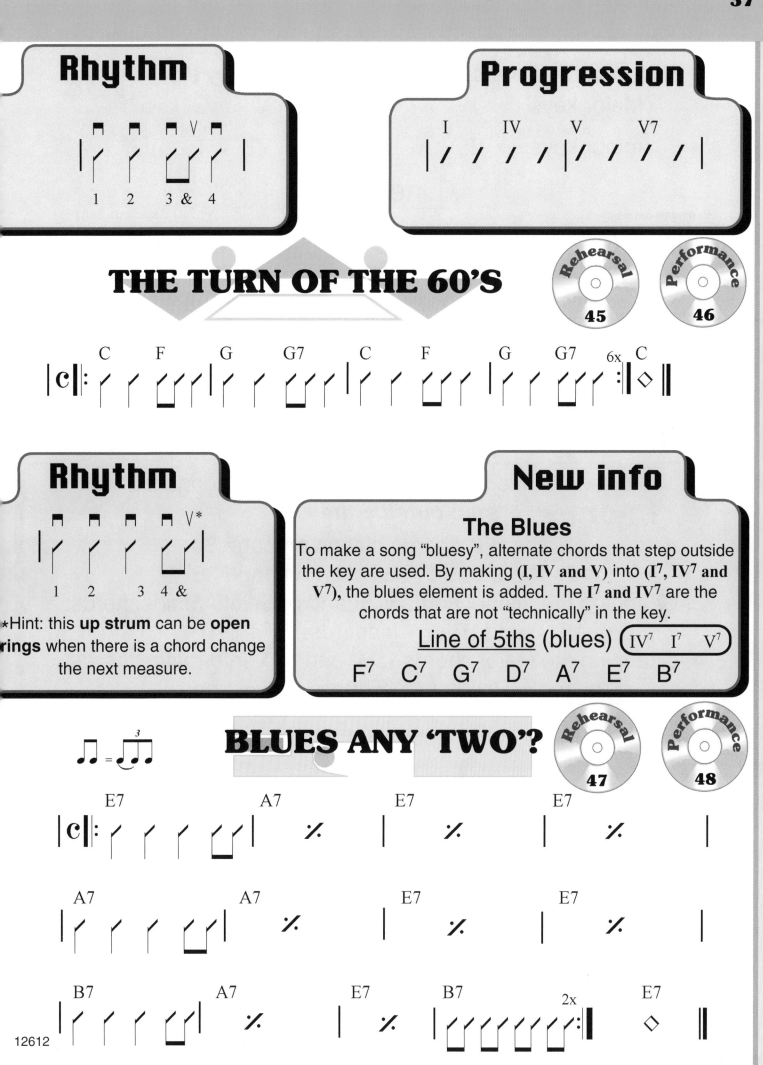

Rhythm

1 2 3 & 4

Progression

I   IV   V   V7

THE TURN OF THE 60'S

Rehearsal 45   Performance 46

C   F   G   G7   C   F   G   G7   6x   C

Rhythm

1 2 3 4 &

*Hint: this **up strum** can be **open rings** when there is a chord change the next measure.

New info

The Blues
To make a song "bluesy", alternate chords that step outside the key are used. By making (I, IV and V) into (I^7, IV^7 and V^7), the blues element is added. The I^7 and IV^7 are the chords that are not "technically" in the key.

Line of 5ths (blues)   (IV^7 I^7 V^7)

F^7 C^7 G^7 D^7 A^7 E^7 B^7

BLUES ANY 'TWO'?

Rehearsal 47   Performance 48

E7   A7   E7   E7

A7   A7   E7   E7

B7   A7   E7   B7   2x   E7

First, review all the chords that are *in each key* **(the rules)**

| Major keys | I | ii | iii | IV | V | vi | vii7$^{♭5}$ |

| minor keys | III | iv | v(V) | VI | VII | **i** | ii7$^{♭5}$ |

Line of 5ths

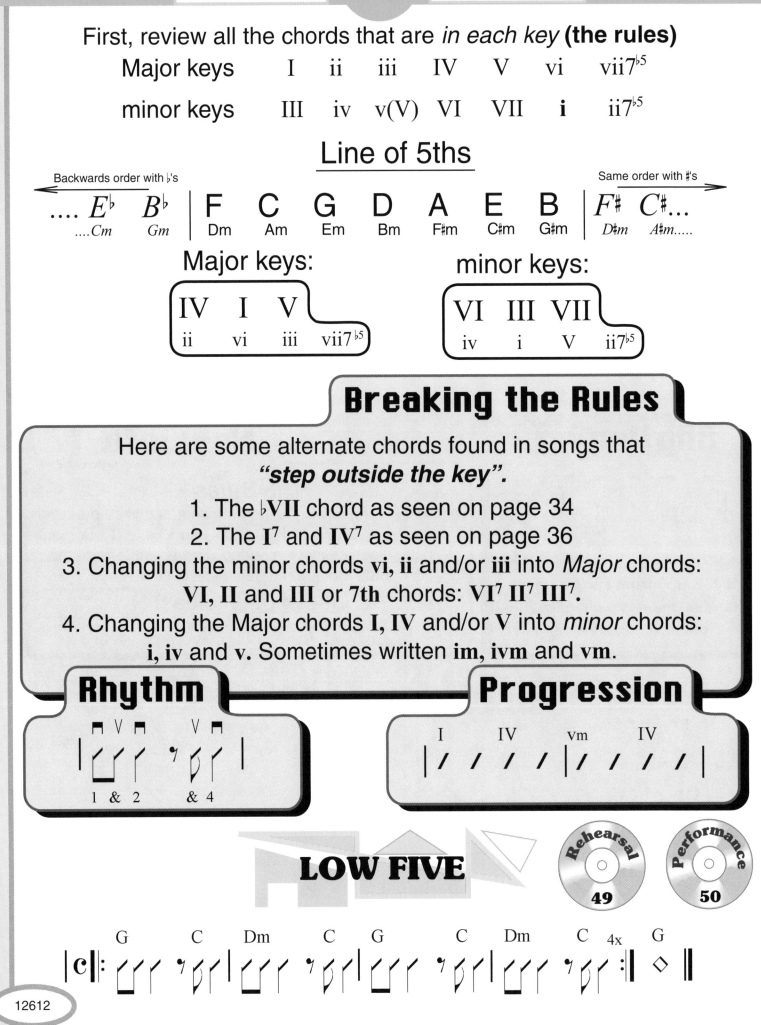

Backwards order with ♭'s ⟵

.... $E^♭$ $B^♭$ | F C G D A E B | $F^♯$ $C^♯$...

....Cm Gm | Dm Am Em Bm F♯m C♯m G♯m | D♯m A♯m.....

⟶ Same order with ♯'s

Major keys:

IV I V

ii vi iii vii7$^{♭5}$

minor keys:

VI III VII

iv i V ii7$^{♭5}$

Breaking the Rules

Here are some alternate chords found in songs that
"step outside the key".

1. The ♭**VII** chord as seen on page 34
2. The **I**^{7} and **IV**^{7} as seen on page 36
3. Changing the minor chords **vi, ii** and/or **iii** into *Major* chords:
VI, II and **III** or 7th chords: **VI^7 II^7 III^7.**
4. Changing the Major chords **I, IV** and/or **V** into *minor* chords:
i, iv and **v.** Sometimes written **im, ivm** and **vm.**

Rhythm

1 & 2   & 4

Progression

I   IV   vm   IV

LOW FIVE

Rehearsal 49   *Performance* 50

G   C   Dm   C   G   C   Dm   C 4x   G

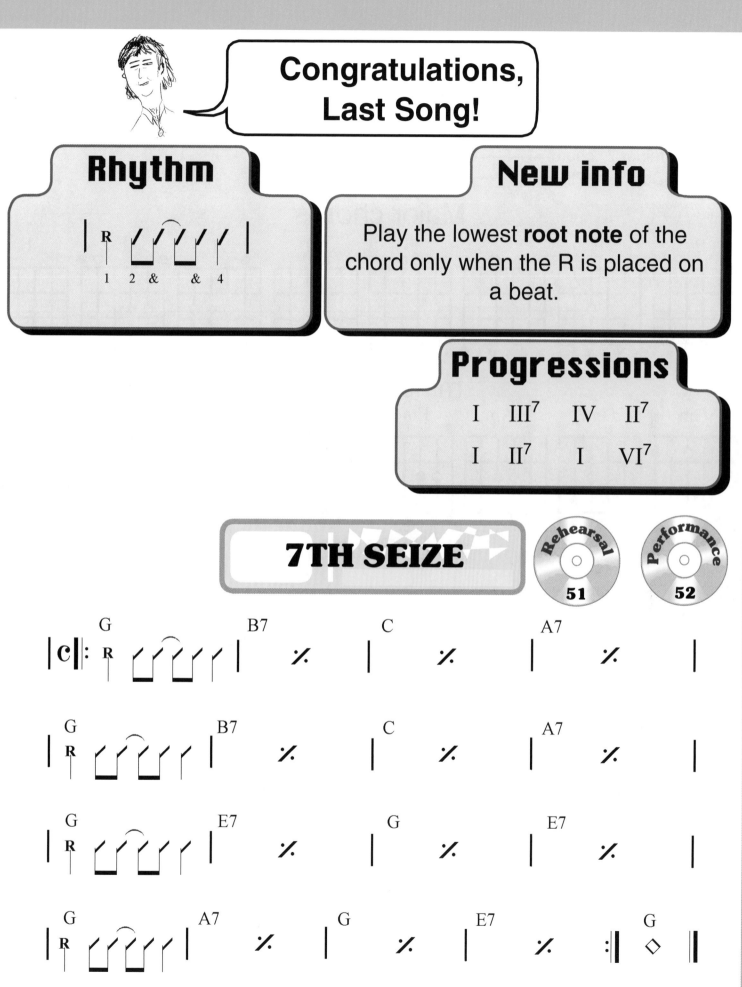

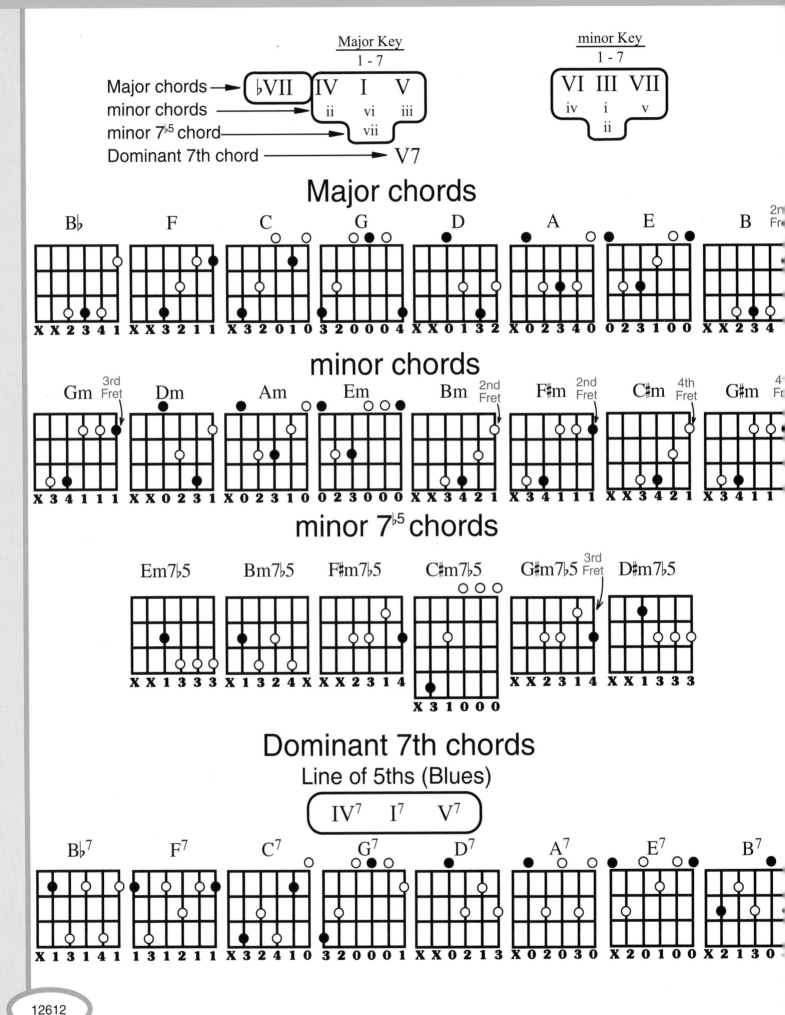